BEST BOOKS

REVIEW BY CHAT GPT

CHAT GPT

Made with ♥ on the Notion Press Platform
www.notionpress.com

I declare that my book is one of the best books out there, and I stand by the quality of its content. It is my firm belief that my book has the power to inspire and transform the lives of readers in profound ways. Through extensive research, thoughtful insights, and engaging storytelling, I have crafted a book that speaks to the heart and soul of readers, providing them with the tools they need to succeed, thrive, and achieve their fullest potential. Whether you're looking to improve your financial well-being, embrace the power of now, or become the hero of your own story, my book is a must-read for anyone looking to make positive changes in their lives. I am confident that my book will leave a lasting impact on readers, and I invite everyone to join me on this journey towards greater fulfillment and happiness.

Contents

Contents

Preface

Books have the power to transport us to new worlds, expand our minds, and connect us with the world around us. They can inspire, educate, and entertain us in ways that few other mediums can. As a lover of books, I have spent countless hours lost in the pages of some of the world's greatest literary works.

This book is a collection of my personal favorites, a list of the best books that I believe everyone should read at least once in their lifetime. These books have had a profound impact on me, shaping the way I see the world and inspiring me to become a better person.

In these pages, you will find a diverse array of genres, from classic literature to modern-day non-fiction. Some of these books may be familiar to you, while others may be entirely new. Regardless of your background or reading preferences, I hope that this book will introduce you to new authors and stories that will capture your imagination and leave a lasting impression.

Above all, my hope is that this book will inspire you to read more, to explore new worlds, and to connect with the incredible power of the written word. So, without further ado, let's dive into the best books that the world has to offer.

CHAPTER I

The Alchemist, by Paulo Coelho

The Alchemist, written by Paulo Coelho, is a remarkable book that tells the story of Santiago, a shepherd boy who embarks on a journey to find his personal legend. This international bestseller has captured the hearts and minds of readers around the world with its timeless wisdom and inspiring message.

At its core, The Alchemist is a fable that explores the nature of destiny and the importance of following one's dreams. Coelho's writing is simple yet powerful, and he weaves a magical tale that is both entertaining and thought-provoking. The story is full of symbolism and metaphors, and it is left up to the reader to interpret their meaning.

One of the strengths of The Alchemist is its accessibility. The book is written in a way that is easy to understand, and its message is universal. Readers of all ages and backgrounds can relate to Santiago's journey and the challenges he faces along the way. The book is also relatively short, making it a quick and enjoyable read.

Another standout feature of The Alchemist is its message of hope and optimism. Santiago's journey is one of self-discovery, and he learns that the universe is conspiring to help him achieve his dreams. This message of positivity is particularly important in today's world, where many people feel disillusioned and uncertain about the future.

Overall, The Alchemist is a timeless classic that deserves its place in the literary canon. Coelho's writing is engaging and inspiring, and the story is full of wisdom and insight. Whether you're looking for a quick read or a life-changing experience, The Alchemist is a book that should not be missed.

CHAPTER II

Rich Dad Poor Dad by Robert Kiyosaki

Rich Dad Poor Dad is a book that has been widely recognized as a game-changer in the world of finance and investing. The book is based on Kiyosaki's personal experience and the teachings of two father figures in his life: his biological father (poor dad) and his best friend's father (rich dad).

The book provides readers with a unique perspective on how to think about money, wealth creation, and financial freedom. It argues that traditional education does not teach individuals how to become financially successful, and that true financial education comes from learning the principles of wealth creation.

Kiyosaki's teachings emphasize the importance of building assets, passive income, and investing in real estate. The book provides practical advice on how to create a mindset shift towards financial success and provides readers with actionable steps they can take to start their journey towards financial freedom.

Overall, Rich Dad Poor Dad is a thought-provoking read that challenges conventional wisdom around money and provides readers with a roadmap towards financial freedom. The book has sold over 32 million copies worldwide and is a must-read for anyone interested in building wealth and achieving financial success.

CHAPTER III

Wings of Fire by Dr. APJ Abdul Kalam

Wings of Fire is an extraordinary autobiography of one of the most inspiring and visionary leaders of India, Dr. APJ Abdul Kalam. The book is a mesmerizing account of his life, achievements, struggles, and aspirations, written in a simple yet engaging style.

The book starts with the early life of Dr. Kalam, growing up in a small village in Tamil Nadu, where he developed an early fascination for science and technology. He recounts his journey from his humble beginnings to his rise as a scientist, his involvement in the development of India's missile program, and his eventual appointment as the President of India.

Throughout the book, Dr. Kalam shares his insights, experiences, and the lessons he learned from his failures and successes. He shares his passion for science, education, and his unwavering belief in the power of youth to transform the world.

What makes this book so unique is the honesty and humility with which Dr. Kalam tells his story. He never shies away from sharing his struggles, failures, and setbacks. He also talks about the impact of his family, friends, and mentors in his life and the importance of having a strong support system.

Wings of Fire is not just a book about a great scientist and leader; it is also a book about hope, determination, and the power of the human spirit. It is a book that will inspire and motivate anyone who wants to make a difference in the world.

Overall, Wings of Fire is an exceptional book that is a must-read for anyone who wants to understand the life and legacy of Dr. APJ Abdul Kalam. It is a book that will leave you with a sense of awe and admiration for this remarkable man and his extraordinary achievements.

CHAPTER IV

The Power of Your Subconscious Mind by Joseph Murphy

"The Power of Your Subconscious Mind" by Joseph Murphy is an insightful and compelling book that explores the incredible power of the human mind. Murphy's book delves deep into the mysteries of the subconscious, showing readers how they can tap into this powerful force to achieve their goals and live a more fulfilling life.

Throughout the book, Murphy uses real-life examples and stories to illustrate the power of the subconscious mind. He shows readers how they can use techniques like visualization, positive affirmations, and meditation to access the subconscious and reprogram it with positive beliefs and attitudes. He also explores the role of the subconscious in manifesting success and abundance in every area of life.

One of the most valuable aspects of "The Power of Your Subconscious Mind" is the practical advice and exercises that Murphy provides throughout the book. From creating a vision board to practicing gratitude, Murphy offers a wide range of tools and techniques that readers can use to harness the power of their subconscious mind.

Overall, "The Power of Your Subconscious Mind" is a must-read for anyone interested in personal growth, self-improvement, or spiritual development. With its clear and concise writing style, practical exercises, and powerful insights, this book is a valuable resource for anyone looking to tap into the limitless potential of their subconscious mind. I highly recommend it to anyone who wants to unlock their full potential and live a more fulfilling life.

CHAPTER V

The Tom Soyar by Mark Twain

"The Tom Soyar" is a novel written by Mark Twain and published in 1876. The book is a classic coming-of-age story that follows the adventures of two young boys, Tom Sawyer and Huckleberry Finn, as they navigate their way through the Mississippi River town of St. Petersburg, Missouri.

The story is set in the mid-19th century and offers an insightful and often humorous look at the social norms and cultural attitudes of the time. Twain expertly captures the essence of boyhood in this novel, with his portrayal of Tom and Huck's mischievous behavior and their desire for freedom and adventure.

One of the most memorable parts of the book is the relationship between Tom and Huck. The two boys come from vastly different backgrounds, with Tom being a mischievous but well-off boy, and Huck being a poor outcast. However, they form an unlikely bond based on their shared love of adventure and their mutual desire to break free from the constraints of their society.

Overall, "The Tom Soyar" is a timeless classic that continues to captivate readers of all ages. Twain's vivid descriptions, engaging characters, and insightful commentary on American culture make this book a must-read for anyone interested in American literature.

CHAPTER VI

The Adventures of Tom Sawyer and Huckleberry Finn by Mark Twain

The Adventures of Tom Sawyer and Huckleberry Finn is a classic novel written by Mark Twain. The book follows the adventures of two young boys, Tom Sawyer and Huckleberry Finn, as they navigate their way through life in a small town on the Mississippi River. The novel is set in the 19th century and provides a glimpse into the social and cultural attitudes of the time.

Tom Sawyer is a mischievous young boy who loves to play pranks and get into trouble. He is a likable character who is both brave and clever. Huck Finn is an orphan who has been taken in by a kind widow and her strict sister. Huck is a free-spirited boy who loves to explore and go on adventures.

The novel is full of humor and excitement, as the two boys embark on various escapades, including treasure hunts, pirate adventures, and getting lost in a cave. Along the way, they learn important life lessons about friendship, loyalty, and the importance of doing what is right.

In conclusion, The Adventures of Tom Sawyer and Huckleberry Finn is a timeless classic that has been enjoyed by generations of readers. It is a must-read for anyone who loves adventure, humor, and a good story.

CHAPTER VII

The Secret by Rhonda Byrne

"The Secret" is a self-help book by Rhonda Byrne that focuses on the law of attraction. The main idea of the book is that people can manifest their desires and dreams by using positive thoughts and visualization techniques. The book offers a step-by-step guide on how to apply the law of attraction in daily life and attract success, wealth, love, and happiness.

The book has been a bestseller since its publication in 2006 and has been translated into over 50 languages. It has also been the subject of controversy and criticism for promoting pseudoscience and the idea that people can control their lives solely through their thoughts.

Overall, "The Secret" offers an interesting perspective on the power of positive thinking and visualization, but it's important to approach it with a critical eye and not rely solely on its teachings for achieving success and happiness.

CHAPTER VIII

Aadujeevitham by Benyamin

"Aadujeevitham" is a Malayalam novel written by Benyamin, a Malayalam writer. The book was published in 2008 and has won several awards including the Kerala Sahitya Akademi Award, the Vayalar Award, and the Crossword Book Award.

The novel tells the story of a young man named Najeeb who leaves his home in Kerala to work in the Gulf. However, he ends up being trapped in a desert and suffers through terrible hardships. The novel explores themes of migration, identity, survival, and redemption.

"Aadujeevitham" has received critical acclaim for its powerful narrative and vivid description of the protagonist's struggles. It has been translated into several languages including English, Tamil, and Hindi.

Overall, "Aadujeevitham" is a must-read for anyone interested in Indian literature, particularly those who want to gain insight into the experiences of migrant workers.

CHAPTER IX

A Brief History of Time by Stephen Hawking

"A Brief History of Time" by Stephen Hawking is a fascinating read that delves into the fundamental questions of the universe. Hawking provides a comprehensive overview of the history of cosmology, beginning with ancient Greek philosophers and ending with the latest scientific theories on black holes and the Big Bang.

The book is written in a way that is accessible to non-scientific readers, yet still manages to delve into complex ideas in a clear and concise manner. Hawking's use of analogies and examples helps to explain some of the more difficult concepts, such as relativity and quantum mechanics.

One of the standout features of "A Brief History of Time" is Hawking's ability to bring a sense of wonder and curiosity to the subject matter. He encourages readers to think beyond their everyday experiences and to imagine what lies beyond our current understanding of the universe.

Overall, "A Brief History of Time" is an excellent read for anyone interested in cosmology or the history of science. Hawking's ability to make complex ideas accessible to a wider audience makes this book a must-read for both scientific and non-scientific readers alike.

CHAPTER X

The Magic by Rhonda Byrne

"The Magic" by Rhonda Byrne is an incredibly inspiring and empowering book that teaches readers how to manifest their desires and transform their lives. This book is a wonderful follow-up to Byrne's previous works, "The Secret" and "The Power," but stands on its own as a powerful guide to unlocking the magic within us all.

In "The Magic," Byrne teaches readers the power of gratitude and how it can transform their lives. By implementing the daily gratitude exercises outlined in the book, readers can start to shift their perspective and focus on the positive aspects of their lives. This in turn, can lead to more abundance, joy, and success.

What sets "The Magic" apart from other self-help books is Byrne's writing style. Her words are uplifting and easy to understand, making the book accessible to readers of all backgrounds. The book is also filled with real-life success stories, which serve as proof of the power of gratitude and manifestation.

Overall, "The Magic" is a must-read for anyone looking to improve their mindset, transform their life, and unlock their full potential. This book is a powerful reminder that we all have the power to create the life we want, and it all starts with gratitude."

CHAPTER XI

The Hero by Rhonda Byrne

"The Hero" by Rhonda Byrne is an incredibly inspiring and thought-provoking book that challenges readers to embrace their inner hero and live their best life. Building on the concepts from her previous works, "The Secret" and "The Power," Byrne encourages readers to harness their own power and potential to become the hero of their own story.

Through a series of essays and exercises, Byrne teaches readers how to identify and overcome the obstacles that hold them back from achieving their goals and living their dreams. She emphasizes the importance of taking action, stepping outside of our comfort zones, and believing in ourselves.

What sets "The Hero" apart from other self-help books is Byrne's emphasis on the power of storytelling. She encourages readers to create their own hero's journey, mapping out the steps they need to take to achieve their goals and overcome their fears. By framing our lives as a hero's journey, we can tap into our own inner strength and overcome even the most daunting challenges.

Overall, "The Hero" is a powerful and uplifting book that offers readers a roadmap to success and personal growth. Byrne's writing style is clear and accessible, making the book a great read for anyone looking to make positive changes in their lives. Whether you're looking to start a new business, overcome a personal challenge, or simply improve your mindset, "The Hero" is a great guide to help you get there."

CHAPTER XII

The Psychology of Money by Morgan Housel

"The Psychology of Money" by Morgan Housel is an eye-opening and thought-provoking book that explores the complex relationship between psychology and money. Housel takes a unique approach to the topic of personal finance, using stories and anecdotes to illustrate the ways in which our emotions and behaviors can impact our financial decisions.

One of the strengths of "The Psychology of Money" is Housel's ability to make complex concepts accessible to readers of all backgrounds. He breaks down financial jargon and presents information in a way that is easy to understand, without ever talking down to his audience.

The book covers a wide range of topics, including the importance of taking a long-term approach to investing, the impact of social norms on our spending habits, and the role of luck in our financial success. Housel also provides a number of practical tips and strategies for readers looking to improve their financial situation.

But what really sets "The Psychology of Money" apart from other personal finance books is its emphasis on the human element of money. Housel recognizes that we are all imperfect creatures with our own biases and blind spots, and that money is not just a matter of numbers and spreadsheets. By understanding our own psychology, we can make better financial decisions and live a more fulfilling life.

Overall, "The Psychology of Money" is an insightful and engaging read that is sure to resonate with anyone looking to improve their financial well-being. Housel's storytelling approach and practical advice make this book a must-read for anyone looking to gain a deeper understanding of the intersection of psychology and money."

CHAPTER XIII

Atomic Habits by James Clear

"Atomic Habits" by James Clear is an outstanding book that provides practical advice for building better habits and breaking bad ones. James Clear's writing style is engaging and accessible, and his insights are backed up by research and real-world examples.

The book is divided into four parts: The Fundamentals of Atomic Habits, The Four Laws of Behavior Change, Make It Obvious, and Make It Attractive. Clear takes readers through a step-by-step process for creating lasting change in their lives, starting with identifying the habits they want to build or break.

Clear's Four Laws of Behavior Change provide a framework for understanding how habits work and how to make lasting changes. By focusing on making habits obvious, attractive, easy, and satisfying, readers can create lasting change in their lives.

One of the strengths of "Atomic Habits" is Clear's emphasis on the importance of small changes. By focusing on making small improvements over time, readers can achieve big results without feeling overwhelmed or discouraged.

Clear's writing is clear and engaging, and he provides numerous real-life examples to illustrate his points. Whether you're looking to improve your health, productivity, or relationships, "Atomic Habits" provides a roadmap for creating lasting change in your life.

Overall, "Atomic Habits" is an excellent read for anyone looking to build better habits and make lasting changes in their lives. Clear's practical advice, engaging writing style, and real-life examples make this book a must-read for anyone looking to achieve their goals and live a more fulfilling life."

CHAPTER XIV

Do It Today by Darius Foroux

"Do It Today" by Darius Foroux is a fantastic guide for anyone looking to improve their productivity and make the most of their time. Foroux's writing style is clear, concise, and easy to understand, making this book an enjoyable and informative read.

The book is divided into short chapters, each one focused on a specific topic related to productivity. Foroux covers everything from goal-setting and time management to decision-making and creativity. One of the strengths of the book is that it provides practical tips and strategies that readers can start implementing immediately. For example, he suggests using a "time block" technique to help manage your schedule, or setting small goals to help build momentum.

What sets "Do It Today" apart from other productivity books is its emphasis on the importance of taking action. Foroux recognizes that simply reading about productivity is not enough – you need to actually do the work. He provides a number of exercises and challenges throughout the book to help readers put his advice into practice.

Another strength of the book is Foroux's emphasis on the mindset behind productivity. He argues that our beliefs and attitudes can have a huge impact on our ability to get things done. By adopting a growth mindset and focusing on progress rather than perfection, we can build resilience and achieve our goals.

Overall, "Do It Today" is a great read for anyone looking to improve their productivity and get more done. Foroux's practical tips, emphasis on action, and focus on mindset make this book a valuable resource for anyone looking to take their productivity to the next level.

CHAPTER XV

Eat That Frog! by Brian Tracy

"Eat That Frog!" by Brian Tracy is a practical and inspiring guide to overcoming procrastination and achieving your goals. The book's title is based on a quote by Mark Twain: "Eat a live frog first thing in the morning, and nothing worse will happen to you the rest of the day." In other words, tackle your most difficult and important task first thing in the morning, and the rest of your day will be a breeze.

The book is divided into 21 chapters, each of which focuses on a different strategy for overcoming procrastination and maximizing productivity. Some of the key strategies include:

Setting clear and specific goals

Breaking down big tasks into smaller, more manageable ones

Prioritizing tasks and focusing on the most important ones

Eliminating distractions and interruptions

Using the "Pareto Principle" (80/20 rule) to focus on the most effective actions

Creating a sense of urgency and taking action immediately

Learning to say "no" to non-essential tasks and requests

Developing positive habits and routines

Tracy's writing style is clear, concise, and easy to understand. He uses real-life examples and anecdotes to illustrate his points, making the book engaging and relatable. The book is also filled with practical tips and exercises that readers can implement right away to improve their productivity.

One of the strengths of "Eat That Frog!" is its emphasis on taking action. Tracy doesn't just provide theoretical advice; he gives readers concrete steps they can take to overcome procrastination and achieve their goals. The book is also focused on long-term success, rather than quick fixes or shortcuts.

Overall, "Eat That Frog!" is an excellent resource for anyone looking to improve their productivity and overcome procrastination. Tracy's strategies are easy to implement and have been proven to be effective in helping people achieve their goals. Whether you're a student, professional, or entrepreneur, this book is a must-read for anyone looking to get more done in less time."

CHAPTER XVI

The Power of Now by Eckhart Tolle

"The Power of Now" by Eckhart Tolle is a life-changing book that challenges readers to live in the present moment and embrace the power of now. This book has become a modern spiritual classic and has inspired millions of readers to let go of their past and future worries and fully embrace the present.

Tolle argues that our minds are constantly preoccupied with thoughts and worries, and that we often forget to live in the present moment. By focusing on the past or future, we miss out on the joy and beauty of the present. Tolle encourages readers to let go of their ego and to connect with their true nature, which is rooted in the present moment.

One of the strengths of "The Power of Now" is Tolle's clear and accessible writing style. He presents complex spiritual concepts in a way that is easy to understand, without ever becoming overly preachy or dogmatic. His writing is engaging and thought-provoking, challenging readers to rethink their approach to life.

The book is filled with practical exercises and meditations that readers can use to connect with the present moment and cultivate a sense of inner peace. Tolle also discusses the impact that our thoughts and emotions have on our lives, and offers guidance on how to detach from negative thought patterns and emotions.

Overall, "The Power of Now" is a profound and insightful book that has the power to transform the way we live our lives. Tolle's emphasis on the importance of living in the present moment is a powerful reminder that we have the power to choose our own happiness and fulfillment. This book is a must-read for anyone looking to cultivate a greater sense of peace and meaning in their lives.

CHAPTER XVII

The Kite Runner by Khaled Hosseini

"The Kite Runner" by Khaled Hosseini is a powerful and emotional novel that explores the complexities of friendship, loyalty, and redemption. Set against the backdrop of Afghanistan's turbulent history, the novel follows the story of Amir, a young boy from Kabul, and his childhood friend Hassan.

The novel begins with a glimpse of Amir's privileged childhood, but soon takes a dark turn as Amir's betrayal of Hassan sets off a chain of events that will haunt him for the rest of his life. As the story unfolds, Amir must confront the demons of his past and find a way to make amends for his mistakes.

One of the strengths of "The Kite Runner" is Hosseini's vivid and evocative writing style. His descriptions of Kabul and its people are richly detailed and paint a vivid picture of a world that is both beautiful and tragic. The novel's characters are also incredibly well-drawn, and the complex relationships between them are explored with great sensitivity and depth.

At its core, "The Kite Runner" is a story about redemption and the power of forgiveness. Amir's journey towards redemption is both moving and inspiring, as he comes to realize that his mistakes cannot be undone, but that he can still make amends for them.

Overall, "The Kite Runner" is a beautifully written and deeply affecting novel that will stay with readers long after they have finished reading. It is a powerful testament to the resilience of the human spirit and the enduring power of friendship and love.

CHAPTER XVIII

Three Idiots by Chetan Bhagat

"Three Idiots" is a heartwarming and entertaining novel by Chetan Bhagat that explores the pressures and expectations placed on students in India's educational system. The book tells the story of three friends, Farhan, Raju, and Rancho, as they navigate the challenges of engineering college and strive to find their true passions in life.

One of the strengths of "Three Idiots" is its relatable characters. Farhan, Raju, and Rancho are three very different individuals with their own unique backgrounds and struggles, but they all share a common desire to break free from the constraints of society and pursue their own dreams. Their friendship is the heart of the book, and their witty banter and hijinks provide plenty of laughs and emotional moments.

The book also highlights the flaws in India's education system and the pressure placed on students to conform to a certain mold. Bhagat's critique of the system is sharp and insightful, and his message of following one's passions and finding joy in learning is an important one.

While the novel is a fun and enjoyable read, it also tackles serious themes such as depression, suicide, and the importance of mental health. Bhagat handles these topics with sensitivity and care, and they add depth and complexity to the story.

Overall, "Three Idiots" is a well-written and thought-provoking novel that will resonate with anyone who has ever felt trapped by societal expectations or struggled to find their place in the world. The book's blend of humor, heart, and social commentary make it a must-read for fans of contemporary fiction.

CHAPTER XIX

“Ikigai: The Japanese Secret to a Long and Happy Life” by Héctor García and Francesc Miralles

"Ikigai: The Japanese Secret to a Long and Happy Life" by Héctor García and Francesc Miralles is a fascinating book that explores the concept of "ikigai," which translates to "the reason for being" in English. Drawing on insights from the Okinawan people, who are known for their longevity and good health, the book offers practical guidance on how to find meaning and purpose in life.

The authors argue that finding one’s ikigai is the key to a long and happy life. Through interviews with centenarians and experts in various fields, the book offers insights into the factors that contribute to a fulfilling life, including a sense of purpose, social connections, and a healthy lifestyle.

One of the strengths of "Ikigai" is its accessibility. The authors present complex concepts in a way that is easy to understand, without ever becoming overly simplistic. The book is filled with practical tips and exercises that readers can use to explore their own ikigai, making it a valuable tool for anyone looking to find greater meaning and purpose in their life.

Another strength of the book is its emphasis on the interconnectedness of the mind, body, and spirit. The authors stress the importance of taking care of oneself in all aspects of life, from diet and exercise to mindfulness and spiritual practice. This holistic approach to wellbeing is both refreshing and inspiring.

Overall, "Ikigai" is a thoughtful and engaging book that offers a unique perspective on the secrets to a long and happy life. The authors' insights into the Okinawan way of life are both inspiring and practical, and the book is sure to leave readers feeling motivated and empowered to find their own ikigai. This book is a must-read for anyone looking to live a more fulfilling life.

CHAPTER XX

I'm OK - You're OK by Thomas A. Harris

"I‘m OK - You’re OK" by Thomas A. Harris is a groundbreaking self-help book that explores the psychology of human interactions and relationships. First published in the 1960s, this book remains a classic in the field of self-help and personal growth.

At the heart of the book is the concept of Transactional Analysis, a form of psychotherapy that emphasizes communication, relationships, and personal growth. Harris argues that every interaction we have with others is a transaction, and that by understanding these transactions, we can improve our relationships and overall well-being.

One of the strengths of "I’m OK - You’re OK" is Harris‘ clear and concise writing style. He presents complex psychological concepts in a way that is easy to understand, using real-world examples to illustrate his points. He also offers practical exercises and strategies that readers can use to improve their communication and relationships.

Another key theme of the book is the importance of self-awareness and personal growth. Harris encourages readers to take responsibility for their own emotions and behaviors, and to work towards becoming their best selves. He also emphasizes the role that empathy and compassion play in building healthy relationships.

Overall, "I’m OK - You’re OK" is a timeless self-help classic that has helped millions of readers improve their communication, relationships, and personal growth.

Harris' insights and strategies are as relevant today as they were when the book was first published, making it a must-read for anyone looking to deepen their understanding of human psychology and improve their relationships.

Printed by Libri Plureos GmbH in Hamburg, Germany